Five-Minute
Bible Devotions

for Children

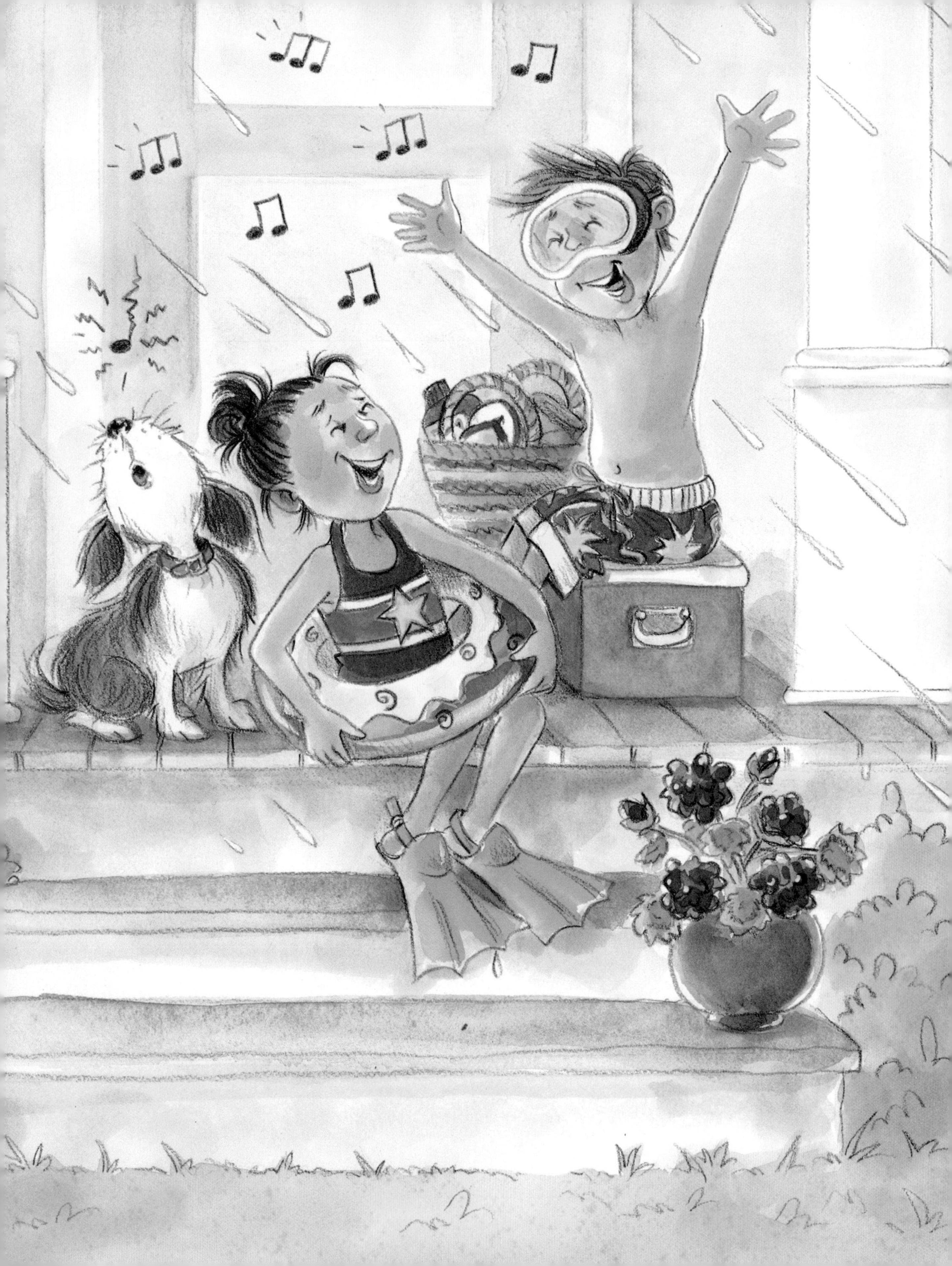

Five-Minute Bible Devotions

for Children

STORIES FROM THE NEW TESTAMENT

Written by Pamela Kennedy and
Anne Kennedy Brady

Illustrated by Amy Wummer

SCHOLASTIC INC.

ISBN 978-0-545-80571-1

12 11 10 9 8 7 6 5 4 3 2 1   14 15 16 17 18 19/0

Printed in the U.S.A.   40

First Scholastic printing, September 2014

Design by Georgina Chidlow-Rucker

For Mattie Rebecca, who taught me to believe. —P.J.K.
For Mom, who taught me to love stories, then gave
me the courage to write my own. —A.K.B.
To Rev. George Palick. —A.W.

Contents

Doing Impossible Things 6

Good News 8

Learning to Obey 10

Good Friends 12

Bullies 14

Teamwork 16

Overcoming Fears 18

Lonely People 20

Choosing to Share 22

Good Neighbors 24

Saying "Sorry" 26

Learning to Pray 28

Sisters and Brothers .30

Saying "Thank You" .32

Doing the Right Thing 34

Alive Forever! 36

Changing for Good 38

Solving Problems 40

Singing Songs 42

Learning and Teaching 44

Family Stories 46

Doing Impossible Things

An Angel Visits Mary (Luke 1:26–39)

One day a young woman named Mary was all alone when an angel appeared to her. She was very surprised! The angel's name was Gabriel, and he said, "Don't be afraid, Mary. God loves you and wants to bless you." Mary listened carefully when Gabriel said, "You will have a baby boy and you will name him Jesus." Then Mary answered, "But I am not married, so how can I have a baby? It's impossible!"

The angel smiled at Mary and said, "Nothing is impossible for God. The baby you will have will be God's only Son." Mary nodded her head and said, "Because I love God, I will trust him and do whatever God wants." Then the angel left Mary, and she ran to tell her family about the miracle God was going to do.

We may not meet an angel like Mary did, but God sends us messages about what he wants us to do through his words in the Bible. God tells us to love others, to forgive people who have been unkind to us, and to share what we have. Sometimes those things are hard to do. But if we love and trust God, he will help us do the right thing, even when it seems impossible.

~~~~~~

Let's talk to God:
Thank you, God, for your words in the Bible that help me know what to do. Please help me to trust you and to be kind and forgiving even when it is hard. Amen.

What do you say?

- In the picture, who is listening to what God says in the Bible?

- What are some things God wants you to do?

- What did Mary say when Gabriel told her she would have a baby boy?

- Why do you think God asks us to do things that may be hard for us to do?

What does God say?

For nothing is impossible with God.

LUKE 1:37

Good News

The Birth of Jesus (Luke 2:1–7,8–20)

Mary married a man named Joseph, and together they traveled to Bethlehem. While they were there, Mary's baby, Jesus, was born. On that same night there were some shepherds living out in the fields, taking care of their sheep. Suddenly, an angel appeared to them, and they were afraid. But the angel said, "Don't be afraid, because I'm here to tell you some good news! Tonight a special baby was born, and he is Christ, the Lord! If you go to Bethlehem, you can see him!" The shepherds were so excited that they hurried to Bethlehem to see if what the angel said was true. There they found Mary, Joseph, and the baby, Jesus, just like the angel said. "This is great news," they said to each other. "Let's tell all our friends so they can come see Jesus too!"

The world is filled with good news. God has made wonderful things like rainbows and mountains, flowers and animals. God hears our prayers and helps us. God gives us families and friends. But the best news is that God loves each one of us very much. When we share this kind of good news with others, it makes them happy, and it helps them trust God too.

Let's talk to God: Thank you, God, for loving me and for sending Jesus to the world. Help me to share this good news with others. Amen.

What do you say?

- In the picture, who looks like he is sharing some good news?

- What was the good news that the shepherds shared?

- What good news can you tell someone you know?

- Why do you think God wants each of us to share good news with others?

What does God say?

I bring you good news that will bring great joy to all people. The Savior . . . has been born today in Bethlehem.
LUKE 2:10B–11

Learning to Obey

The Boy Jesus at the Temple (Luke 2:41–52)

When Jesus was twelve years old, he traveled with his parents to the city of Jerusalem to celebrate the feast of the Passover. When the feast was over, Mary and Joseph and the others started back home to Nazareth. They thought that Jesus was with them, but he was not! When his parents realized that Jesus was not with them, they hurried back to Jerusalem to find him. They looked all day until they finally found him in the temple.

"Why didn't you come with us when we left?" Mary asked. "We were so afraid!" Jesus said, "Don't worry, Mother. I was right here in God's temple talking to the teachers."

"You need to come home with us now," said Mary. Jesus loved his parents. He left the temple and went with Mary and Joseph. Jesus obeyed his parents and grew up to be strong and wise.

It is fun to learn how to do things by ourselves. But even though we can do lots of things, we still need to listen to our parents and do what they say. Because they love us, they want to help us grow up to be strong and wise. And when we obey our parents, we show them that we love them too.

Let's talk to God: Dear God, thank you for giving me parents who love me and take care of me. Please help me to obey my parents and to grow up to be strong and wise. Amen.

What do you say?

- Can you name some things that the kids in the picture have learned to do?

- What did Jesus do after his parents found him in the temple?

- What are some ways that you obey your parents?

- Why do you think God wants children to obey their parents?

What does God say?

Children, obey your parents because you belong to the Lord, for this is the right thing to do.

EPHESIANS 6:1

Good Friends

Jesus Chooses Twelve Disciples (Matthew 4:18–22; Mark 3:13–19; Luke 6:12–16)

When Jesus grew up, he left his family to do the work God had planned for him. He knew that he would need good friends, so he asked twelve other men to help him. These special friends were called disciples. They traveled with Jesus, and together they learned many things. Jesus taught them about God, and they told other people about what Jesus said. They ate their meals, walked, and talked together. They listened to each other and shared good times and bad times. When Jesus needed help, they helped him; and when they were sad or afraid, Jesus helped them. Jesus and his disciples loved each other and took good care of each other because that is what good friends do.

Just like Jesus and his disciples, we all need good friends. Good friends enjoy having fun together. When we are sad or afraid, a good friend can listen to us and help us feel better. Good friends don't say mean things to each other or try to get their friends into trouble. Instead, they think about ways to make each other happy and help each other do the right thing.

~~~~~~

Let's talk to God: Dear God, I am so glad that you love me and have given me good friends. Please help me to be a good friend to others, to listen to them, and to be kind. Amen.

What do you say?

- Can you count the friends who are playing a game together?

- How many disciples did Jesus choose to be his best friends?

- Who are some of your good friends, and what do you enjoy doing together?

- Why do you think God wants us to have good friends?

What does God say?

This is my commandment: Love each other in the same way I have loved you.
JOHN 15:12

Bullies

Jesus Silences the Pharisees (John 8:2–11)

One day when Jesus was teaching in the temple, a group of important men called Pharisees came to see him. They brought a woman with them, and they made her stand in front of Jesus. Then they pointed to her and said, "This woman broke our rules. We think she should be punished. What do you think?"

Jesus didn't say anything for a while. He looked at the woman. Then he looked at the men. Finally Jesus said, "If any one of you has never done anything wrong, you can be the first to punish her." One by one, the Pharisees walked away. When they were all gone, Jesus looked at the woman. He said, "Look, those bullies have all gone away, and you are free to go too. I forgive you for what you did wrong. Try to do the right thing from now on."

The Pharisees who brought the woman to Jesus were bullying her. Bullying means to do or say things that are mean and hurtful. Jesus doesn't want us to bully each other, because he cares about each of us—even when we make mistakes. If you know that someone is hurting other people or if you are afraid that they will hurt you, then you should tell a teacher, a parent, or another grown-up right away. When you report bullying, you are helping to keep everyone safe.

Let's talk to God:
Thank you, God, for loving each of us so much. Please help me to be a good friend. Give me courage to speak up if someone is being bullied. Amen.

What do you say?

- Can you find the grown-up in the picture?

- Who was bullying the woman in the story?

- What should you do if someone is bullying others?

- Why do you think Jesus does not like bullying?

What does God say?

Speak up for those who cannot speak for themselves.
PROVERBS 31:8A

Teamwork

Jesus Heals a Paralyzed Man (Mark 2:1–12)

Four friends lived in a town called Capernaum. They had another friend who couldn't walk, but they wanted to take him to see Jesus. How could they get him there? They decided to put their friend on a cot, and together they carried him all the way to the house where Jesus was teaching. But when they got there, the house was so crowded with people that they couldn't even get near the door. "I have a plan!" one said. They worked together to get their friend up on the roof! Then they carefully removed part of the roof and lowered their friend down until he was right in front of Jesus. Jesus was surprised and happy that everyone had worked together. He healed the sick man, and the man left the house praising God.

God knows we want to do big things, but sometimes a job is too hard for us to do by ourselves. That is one reason God gives us friends. When we work together, we can do things that we could never do alone. Working together is called "teamwork." As part of a team, we can share ideas and solve problems. We can break a big job into little jobs so everyone can help. Next time you have a problem you can't solve or you want to do something big, try working with others. You will be surprised at what you can do together!

Let's talk to God: Thank you, God, for good friends. Please help me learn to work with others so I can do big things! Amen.

What do you say?

- In the picture, who is using teamwork?

- How did the friends in the story help each other?

- Tell about a time when you used teamwork.

- Why do you think it makes God happy when we work together?

What does God say?

Two people are better off than one, for they can help each other succeed.

ECCLESIASTES 4:9

Overcoming Fears

Jesus Calms the Storm (Matthew 8:23–27)

Jesus and his disciples were sailing across a big lake. Suddenly, the clouds got dark and it started to rain. It rained harder and harder. The wind blew, and huge waves crashed into the boat. The disciples were terrified! What if they fell overboard? What if their boat sank? But Jesus was sleeping peacefully. They woke him up and cried, "Please help us! This storm is going to sink our boat!" Jesus told them, "Don't be afraid. Have faith in what I can do." Then he stood up in the boat and ordered the wind and the sea to be calm. Immediately, the sky cleared, the wind was quiet, and the waves disappeared. The disciples were amazed. "Look how powerful Jesus is," they said. "Even the wind and the waves do what he says!"

Everyone feels afraid sometimes. We might feel afraid when it's dark or if there's a big storm outside. It can be scary to try something new. But God isn't afraid of anything! God has promised to take care of us, and he always keeps his promises. If you feel afraid, try praying and telling God how you feel. He loves each one of us very much, and when we tell him how we feel, he can remind us that he is always with us. He is much stronger than anything that frightens us.

Let's talk to God: Dear God, thank you for promising to protect me. Sometimes I get scared, but I know you're not scared of anything. Please help me whenever I feel afraid. Amen.

What do you say?

- What do you think might be scary in the picture?

- Why were Jesus' disciples afraid?

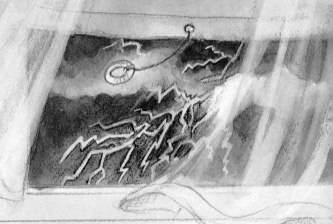

- What does it feel like when you get scared?

- Why do you think talking to God can make you feel better when you're afraid?

What does God say?

Don't be afraid . . . for you are very precious to God.
Daniel 10:19a

Lonely People

Jesus Talks to the Woman at the Well (John 4:4–30)

Jesus was traveling through a country called Samaria. It was very hot, so Jesus sat down to rest by a well. A woman came to the well to get some water, and Jesus asked, "Will you please give me a drink of water?" The woman was surprised. "Most people don't want to talk to me. Why are you different?" Jesus said, "Because I care about you, and I want you to know how much God loves you."

The woman did not think God would love her. No one else in her town wanted to be her friend because she had made some bad choices. Jesus saw how lonely she was. He told her he was God's Son, he knew everything about her, and that God loved her. Then she knew she didn't have to be lonely anymore. The woman was so happy that she ran to share the good news with everyone in her town. "God's Son has come at last!" she told them.

Do you know people who seem lonely? Maybe they are different or it is hard for them to learn new things. They might not have many friends, and other kids might tease them. Remember that God loves everyone and wants us to share his love with others. So if you see someone getting teased or left out, try being kind to that person. You'll make God very happy, and you might find a new friend too!

Let's talk to God:
Jesus, thank you for showing me how to love people. Please help me be kind to those who are different from me, and to help people who are lonely. Amen.

What do you say?

- Who in the picture looks sad?

- Why was the woman in the story surprised that Jesus talked to her?

- Can you think of someone who might need a friend?

- Why do you think God cares about lonely people?

What does God say?

Show mercy and kindness to one another.
ZECHARIAH 7:9B

Choosing to Share

Jesus Feeds the Five Thousand (John 6:1–15)

One day Jesus and his friends went up to a hilly place and sat down on the ground. Soon, lots of people gathered around. They all wanted to be close to Jesus, because he was powerful and could do miracles. It was almost dinnertime, so Jesus said to his friends, "You should give these people something to eat." But his friends said, "We don't have any food, and there are so many people to feed. It's impossible!"

One of Jesus' friends named Andrew said, "All we can find is a boy with five small loaves of bread and two little fish. That's not enough to do any good." But the boy chose to share his food anyway, and Jesus thanked God for it. Then a miracle happened. When Jesus gave out the boy's bread and fish, there was enough for more than five thousand people! There were even leftovers! God took what the little boy shared and used it to bless everyone there.

The boy in the Bible story did not have very much, but he still made a choice to share it. Sometimes we choose not to share because we want to keep everything for ourselves. Maybe we are afraid to lose what we have. But this story shows us that when we choose to share, we not only help others, but God gives us blessings too. When we share, we show that we trust God to take care of us.

Let's talk to God: Thank you, God, for giving me so much. Please help me to choose to share the things I have with others. Amen.

What do you say?

- Who in the picture is choosing to share?

- What did the boy in the Bible story choose to share?

- Talk about a time when you shared something.

- Why do you think God wants us to share what we have?

What does God say?

Don't forget to do good and to share with those in need.
HEBREWS 13:16A

Good Neighbors

The Good Samaritan (Luke 10:25–37)

Someone asked Jesus how to get to heaven. Jesus said, "You must love God and also love your neighbor." Then the man asked, "But who *is* my neighbor?" So Jesus told a story: "A man was traveling alone when robbers grabbed him, beat him up, and stole everything he had. Then they left him lying at the side of the road. After a while, a priest came along, saw the man, but did not help him. Later, a worker from the Temple came by. When he saw the hurt man, he kept right on walking! Finally, a Samaritan, a person nobody liked, came down the road. When he saw the beaten man, he felt sorry for him. The Samaritan comforted the man, then he lifted him onto his donkey and took him into town. There he bought food and medicine to help the hurt man get better."

Jesus asked, "Who was a good neighbor?" The person who heard the story said, "It was the Samaritan, because he was helpful and kind." Jesus said, "That's right! You should try to be just like him."

Sometimes we think our neighbors are just the people we know. But Jesus teaches us that anyone who needs help or kindness is our neighbor. When we take time to look around and see who is hurt or sad and then we choose to help them, we are doing what Jesus said to do. We are being a good neighbor!

Let's talk to God: Dear God, help me see when someone is sad or hurting. Then show me how to be a good neighbor to them. Amen.

What do you say?

• Who in the picture is being a good neighbor?

• How did the Samaritan show he was a good neighbor?

• How has someone been a good neighbor to you?

• Why do you think Jesus wants you to be a good neighbor?

What does God say?

Love your neighbor as yourself.
LUKE 10:27B

Saying "Sorry"

The Story of the Lost Son (Luke 15:11–32)

Jesus told a story about a son who ran away from home. For a while it was fun to do whatever he wanted. But before long he got into trouble and ran out of money. He was lonely and so poor that he was eating with pigs! He missed his family, and he felt ashamed and afraid. He wanted to go home, but what if his father didn't love him anymore? As he started the long walk home, he worried about what his father would say. While he was still a long way off, his father saw him and ran to him. The son begged, "Father, I'm sorry I ran away. If I promise to be your servant, will you let me come home?" The father gave him a big hug. "You will always be my son!" he said. "Welcome home!"

When we make bad choices, it isn't always easy to say we're sorry. We may feel scared that people won't like us anymore. But Jesus loves us no matter what. He tells us that making a bad choice doesn't mean someone is a bad person. In fact, mistakes can help us learn to make better choices next time. But first, Jesus tells us, it's important to admit when we do something wrong. Doing this shows that we want to do better. Good friends say "I'm sorry," then they try not to hurt each other again.

Let's talk to God: Dear God, thank you for loving me, even when I make bad choices. Please help me say "I'm sorry" when I've hurt someone, and help me make good choices instead. Amen.

What do you say?

- In the picture, who looks like he might be sorry?

- Why was the son in the story afraid to go home?

- Talk about a time you needed to say "I'm sorry."

- Why do you think God wants us to say "I'm sorry" to each other?

What does God say?

Confess your sins to each other and pray for each other.

JAMES 5:16A

Learning to Pray

The Lord's Prayer (Matthew 6:5–13; Luke 11:1–4)

One of Jesus' followers came to him and asked, "Will you teach us how to pray?" Jesus said, "Yes, I will. First of all, don't pray just to show off. When you pray, talk to God in private. And don't keep saying the same thing over and over. God knows what you need, but he wants you to tell him about it in your own words." Then Jesus prayed the kind of prayer he was talking about. We call it "The Lord's Prayer."

You might like to memorize the words of The Lord's Prayer, found in Matthew 6:9–13. But you can also make up your own prayers. Here is a fun way to do that: Think of the four letters in the word *PRAY*.

P is for Praise. Praise God for his goodness and love.
R is for Remember. Remember how God has helped you, and thank him.
A is for Ask. Ask God to help others, to keep your family safe, or comfort a friend.
Y is for You! Tell God what you wonder about, and ask him for what you need.

God loves you very much, and he can't wait to hear what you're thinking about. So remember to P.R.A.Y. every day!

~~~~~~

Let's talk to God: Thank you, Jesus, for teaching me how to pray. I am glad you care about the things that matter to me. Please help me remember to praise you every day. Amen.

What do you say?

- Who in the picture is praying?

- What do we call the special prayer Jesus taught his followers?

- What are some things you want to pray about?

- Why do you think prayer is important to God?

The Lord is my Shepherd

What does God say?

Pray about everything. Tell God what you need, and thank him for all he has done.

PHILIPPIANS 4:6B

Sisters and Brothers

Mary and Martha (Luke 10:38–42)

Jesus had been walking and teaching for a long time. He was tired and hungry, so he went to the house of some friends. They invited him to come in and stay for dinner. There were two sisters living at the house. Their names were Mary and Martha. Mary loved Jesus and wanted to hear what he had to say, so she sat near him and listened to him teach about God. Martha also loved Jesus, so she ran right to the kitchen to fix him some dinner. After a while, Martha got angry because Mary wasn't helping her in the kitchen. Martha went to Jesus and said, "My sister isn't doing anything! I'm doing all the work! Tell her to help me!" But Jesus said, "Martha, don't be so worried. Don't be upset. What Mary is doing is important too. She's listening to my words."

Sometimes we feel upset when a sister or a brother gets more attention than we do. Maybe we feel left out. We might even get angry like Martha did and say something like: "Look at me. What I'm doing is better." Brothers and sisters don't always do things the same way. But in a family there is always plenty of love for every person. When we look for ways to get along with one another it makes the whole family happier.

Let's talk to God: Thank you, Lord, for each person in my family. Please help me to show them how much I love them every day. Amen.

What do you say?

- In the picture, what kinds of different things are the brothers and sisters doing?

- Why was Martha upset with her sister?

- Can you talk about some of the ways the people in your family are different from one another?

- Why do you think Jesus wants brothers, sisters, and parents to all get along together?

What does God say?

How wonderful and pleasant it is, when brothers [and sisters] live together in harmony!
PSALM 133:1

Saying "Thank You"

The Ten Lepers (Luke 17:11–19)

One day Jesus and his friends came to a small town. As soon as they entered the town, they saw ten sick men standing together. The men had heard that Jesus could make people well, so they called out, "Jesus, Master, please help us!" Jesus looked at them and told them to go to the temple. This seemed like a strange command, but as the men did what Jesus said, their sickness went away. All ten of them were well again. Then one of the men came back to Jesus and knelt down.

"Oh, Jesus, thank you for making me well," he said.

Jesus asked, "Weren't there ten sick men who were healed? Why did only one come back to say thank you to God?" Then Jesus gave a special blessing to the man who was thankful.

Saying "thank you" is a way of showing God how glad we are for all his blessings. He makes beautiful stars to shine at night and sunshine and rain so flowers and trees can grow. He gives us friends and family to love. When we get hurt, God helps us get better. And best of all, God sent Jesus to show us how to live. God gives us all the good things we enjoy and it makes him happy when we take time to say "thank you."

Let's talk to God: Dear God, thank you for making every good thing, for helping me each day, and for loving me forever. Amen.

What do you say?

- Can you name some of the things in the picture that are blessings from God?

- In the story, how many men came back to thank Jesus for making them well?

- What are some things you are thankful for?

- Why do you think it makes God happy when we say "thank you" to him?

What does God say?

Give thanks to the LORD, for he is good!

PSALM 107:1A

Doing the Right Thing

Jesus Visits Zacchaeus' House (Luke 19:1–10)

Jesus was coming to visit the town of Jericho. Excited people filled the streets. A rich man named Zacchaeus wanted to see Jesus, but he was too short to see over the crowds. So he found a tree and quickly climbed it. When Jesus came by, he stopped under the tree and looked up. "Zacchaeus, come down right now! I want to stay at your house today," he said. Everyone was surprised. Most people in Jericho didn't like Zacchaeus because he had become rich by stealing money from them. Why would Jesus want to spend time with him? But Zacchaeus scrambled down and invited Jesus to his home for dinner.

After they ate, Zacchaeus stood up and said, "I want to give half of my money to help the poor. And I will also give back four times what I have stolen from people." Jesus said, "This shows that you are sorry for doing wrong. I'm happy you have chosen to do the right thing." Zacchaeus was glad too.

Sometimes we make bad choices. We say unkind words. We take things that are not ours. We tell lies. God knows all about our mistakes, and he wants to help us do what is right instead. This is not always easy. But when we choose to do the right thing, we feel better and it makes Jesus happy too.

~~~~~~

Let's talk to God: Dear God, when I make mistakes, please help me to be brave enough to choose to do the right thing. Amen.

What do you say?

- Who in the picture looks like he might have made a bad choice?

- What good choices did Zacchaeus make?

- Talk about a time when you chose to do the right thing.

- Why do you think God wants us to do the right thing?

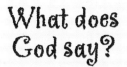

What does God say?

But even if you suffer for doing what is right, God will reward you for it.

1 PETER 3:14A

Alive Forever!

The Resurrection (Matthew 26–28; Mark 14–16; Luke 22–24; John 18–20)

Jesus' friends were very sad. Some bad people had nailed Jesus to a wooden cross. Then they had watched while he died. Afterwards, two of Jesus' friends took his body down from the cross and gently wrapped it in cloth. They put his body in a small rock cave called a tomb. They put a huge stone in front of the tomb to close it. Three days after Jesus died, the women who were his friends brought some sweet-smelling spices to put into the tomb with Jesus' body. When they got to the tomb, they saw that the huge stone was pushed away. Then they peeked inside and saw that Jesus' body was gone! Suddenly, two bright, shining angels appeared. They said, "Jesus isn't here. He is alive!" Even though the bad people tried to get rid of Jesus, God was more powerful. God raised Jesus from the dead, and now Jesus is alive in heaven forever!

We remember this wonderful story from the Bible every year when we go to church on Easter Sunday. But do you know what else the Bible tells us? Because Jesus died on the cross and came to life again, everyone who believes in Jesus can go to heaven after they die too. Now we do not need to be afraid to die, because we know that when we go to heaven we will live with Jesus forever!

~~~~~~

Let's talk to God: Thank you, Jesus, for loving me so much. I trust in you and thank you for making a home for me in heaven. Amen.

What do you say?

• Can you count all the people who are going to church?

• What did the angels tell the women who came to the tomb?

• What do you think heaven will be like?

• Why do you think God wants us to live with Jesus forever?

What does God say?

For we know that . . . (when we die and leave this earthly body), we will have a house in heaven.

2 CORINTHIANS 5:1A

Changing for Good

Saul is Converted (Acts 9:1–22)

A man named Saul was angry because people said Jesus was God's Son. He told them to stop teaching about Jesus, but they would not. So Saul chased them out of their homes and even put them in jail. Then one day as Saul traveled to the town of Damascus, Jesus appeared to him in a bright light.

"Why are you being so mean, Saul?" Jesus asked. Saul was so scared he fell to the ground. "Who are you?" he cried. Then Jesus said, "I'm Jesus. Get up, go into town, and wait." So Saul did what Jesus said.

After three days, Jesus sent a man named Ananias to Saul with a special message: "Jesus wants you to change. Stop hurting people. Tell them how much Jesus loves them instead." Saul believed Jesus' message. And he decided to follow Jesus for the rest of his life! God changed Saul's heart for good. He even called him by a new name: Paul.

Some people are like Saul. They do not know how much God loves them. They may even do things that hurt others. But the Bible says that when we choose to believe in Jesus, he promises to help us change for good. When God helps us, just like Saul, we want to tell others about God's love for them too.

Let's talk to God: Thank you, Jesus, for loving me. Please help me to change for good, to follow you, and to share your love with others. Amen.

What do you say?

- Who is showing God's love to someone else?

- How did Saul change for good?

- Who would you like to tell about God's love?

- Why do you think Jesus wants people to know that he loves them?

What does God say?

Anyone who belongs to Christ has become a new person. The old life is gone; a new life has begun!

2 CORINTHIANS 5:17B

Solving Problems

Paul and Barnabas Disagree (Acts 15:36–41)

Paul and Barnabas were good friends. They traveled together telling people about Jesus. One day Barnabas said he wanted to bring along his cousin John Mark, who had traveled with them before but left when the work got too hard. Paul didn't want to take John Mark with them, and Paul and Barnabas argued. Finally they found a way to solve their problem. "We will not travel together for a while," they said. So Barnabas took John Mark and headed in one direction, and Paul took a friend named Silas and went in a different direction. Now twice as many people would hear about Jesus!

Even good friends don't always think alike. It's easy to feel angry when your friend doesn't agree with you. A simple disagreement can turn into a big fight. Feelings may get hurt, and sometimes people even stop being friends. God doesn't want disagreements to end friendships. He wants us to work together to solve problems. So if you don't agree with something your friend says or does, try talking about it. You might have to give up a little of what you want, and your friend might have to do the same. But by talking things through, you can make your friendship stronger, and you might even discover a way to do things that is better than you imagined!

Let's talk to God: Dear God, thank you for my friends. Please help me speak kindly, even if I feel like arguing. And please help me find good ways to solve problems. Amen.

What do you say?

- What does the boy in the picture want?

- Tell about a time you and a friend disagreed about something.

- Why did Paul and Barnabas disagree?

- Why does God want us to talk about disagreements?

What does God say?

A servant of the Lord must not quarrel but must be kind to everyone.

2 TIMOTHY 2:24A

Singing Songs

Paul and Silas in Jail (Acts 16:16–34)

Paul and his friend Silas traveled together teaching about Jesus. Many people enjoyed listening to them. But others did not like to hear about Jesus and wanted Paul and Silas to go away. One day, in a town called Philippi, Paul prayed for a young slave girl to be healed. God answered the prayer, but the owners of the slave girl were angry. They went to the town leaders. "Paul and Silas are breaking the law. You should punish them!" So the town leaders took Paul and Silas and locked them in jail. But Paul and Silas trusted that God would take care of them. Do you know what they did? In the middle of the night, even though they were in a dark prison cell, they prayed and sang songs to God!

Have you ever felt sad or alone or afraid? What did you do? Sometimes it helps if we talk to God about how we are feeling. When we talk to God we call it prayer. We can tell God why we are sad or what is making us afraid. He always listens. Another thing we can do is to sing. Sometimes singing a song can help us feel better. A song such as "Jesus Loves Me" reminds us that God always cares for us.

Let's talk to God: Dear Lord, I love you, and I thank you for loving me. Help me to sing songs to you every day. Amen.

What do you say?

- How many people in the picture are singing?

- What did Paul and Silas do when they were in the jail?

- Why do you think God likes it when we pray and sing songs to him?

- What kinds of songs help you feel better?

What does God say?

I will sing of your love and justice, LORD. I will praise you with songs.
PSALM 101:1

Learning and Teaching

Priscilla and Aquila Teach Apollos (Acts 18:1–4, 18–28)

Priscilla and her husband, Aquila, were Paul's friends. Whenever Paul visited the city where they lived, he stayed at their house and taught them more about Jesus. Priscilla and Aquila listened to Paul and learned many new things. Then they taught others what they had learned from Paul. One day a new teacher named Apollos came to the town of Ephesus. Priscilla and Aquila went to hear him. He was a good teacher, but there were some things he did not know about Jesus. So Priscilla and Aquila taught him the things they had learned from Paul. Apollos was glad he had learned new things about Jesus and began to teach others what he had learned.

When you were first born, you could not do very much. The people who loved you taught you how to clap your hands and how to crawl. Then they helped you learn to walk and talk. Before long you could do many new things. When you were older maybe you learned how to write your name, read a book, tie your shoes, or jump rope. You have to be a good listener to learn something new, and then you must practice it over and over before you can do it well. But once you learn something, it is fun to teach it to someone else. We all grow up by being both learners and teachers.

Let's talk to God: Dear God, thank you for giving me good teachers. Help me to learn well so I can teach others too. Amen.

What do you say?

- In the picture, who is being a learner? Who is being a teacher?

- What is something you have learned that you can teach to someone else?

- What did Apollos learn from Priscilla and Aquila?

- Why is it important to be both a learner *and* a teacher?

What does God say?

The tongue of the wise makes knowledge appealing.

PROVERBS 15:2A

Family Stories

Examples of Faith (Hebrews 11:4–40)

The Bible contains letters written to many different groups of people. One of these letters is called Hebrews. The writer wanted the Hebrew people to understand more about faith, or trusting God. So he told them stories about people in their family who had lived long ago. He chose stories about people who believed God's promises and were able to do great things. He talked about Noah, who built a huge boat that saved his family and all kinds of animals from a great flood. He reminded them that Moses led the people as they left Egypt and traveled through the Red Sea. And he told how God blessed a brave woman named Rahab because she helped men who were fighting for God! These and other stories helped the Hebrews understand more about their families, and more about trusting God too.

Storybooks are fun to read. But did you know your parents and grandparents have lots of true stories to share? They can tell you about things they did when they were little or about how God helped them through a difficult time. They might even share funny stories. It's fun to hear about family history, especially because it's about people you know. Why not ask your parents or grandparents to tell you their favorite family story? They will love sharing it, and you might learn some very interesting things!

~~~~~~

Let's talk to God: Dear God, thank you for my family. Help me to be a good listener when they tell stories, and to learn from them. Amen.

What do you say?

• Can you find the grandparent in the picture?

• What letter in the Bible has stories about Noah, Moses, and Rahab?

• What is one of your favorite family stories?

• Why do you think family stories are important to God?

What does God say?

What you learn from [your parents] will crown you with grace.

PROVERBS 1:9A

K.M. Kennedy

ANNE AND PAMELA

Pamela Kennedy loves writing for children and has authored more than thirty books, including *Five-Minute Bible Devotions for Children: Stories from the Old Testament*. In her spare time she enjoys hiking, reading, and exploring the beaches of Puget Sound. Pam and her husband currently live in Seattle, Washington.

Anne Kennedy Brady is an actress and writer in Chicago. When the stage and the laptop are dark, she enjoys rock climbing and long city walks with her husband in search of the perfect deep dish pizza.

Mark Wummer

AMY

Amy Wummer is an award-winning illustrator with over fifty children's books to her credit. Her lively watercolor illustrations for *Five-Minute Bible Devotions for Children* help kids relate to the New Testament stories. She and her husband, Mark, have three grown children and live in Pennsylvania.